W9-BLR-518

NATURE CLOSE-UP

JUNIORS

Soil

TEXT BY ELAINE PASCOE

PHOTOGRAPHS BY DWIGHT KUHN

BLACKBIRCH PRESS

An imprint of Thomson Gale, a part of The Thomson Corporation

THOMSON

GALE

Detroit • New York • San Francisco • San Diego • New Haven, Conn. • Waterville, Maine • London • Munich

THOMSON

✳

™

GALE

For more information, contact
Blackbirch Press
27500 Drake Rd.
Farmington Hills, MI 48331-3535
Or you can visit our Internet site at http://www.gale.com

Photo Credits: All pages © Dwight R. Kuhn Photography

LIBRARY OF CONGRESS CATALOGING-IN-PUBLICATION DATA

Pascoe, Elaine.
  Soil / by Elaine Pascoe.
      p. cm. — (Nature close-up jr.)
  Includes bibliographical references and index.
  ISBN 1-4103-0311-X (hard cover : alk. paper)
  1. Soils—Juvenile literature. 2. Soil ecology—Juvenile literature. 3. Soils—Experiments
—Juvenile literature. 4. Soil ecology—Experiments—Juvenile literature. I. Title II. Series:
Pascoe, Elaine. Nature close-up junior.

  S591.3.P37 2004
  577.5'7—dc22

                                                                                2004013975

Printed in China
10 9 8 7 6 5 4 3 2 1

Contents

Read this first:

Have fun when you look for wildlife, but be smart. Take an adult with you. Walk carefully. Don't bother the animals that you see—just enjoy them.

Where can you find wildlife? You may not have to look very far. You may find all sorts of living things in the soil right under your feet!

The soil is not just dirt. It is a home, or **habitat,** for plants and animals. The plants send their roots into the soil. Animals dig and tunnel in the soil. The plants and animals depend on each other. Together, they form a community.

Much of the life in soil is out of sight. It is hidden, but you can find it if you know where to look.

A new pumpkin plant grows roots in soil.

Plants and Soil

Lots of plants grow in soil. A plant's roots are like anchors. They hold the plant in place. The roots of a big tree grow deep in the soil. A small plant's roots are close to the surface.

Plant roots have another important job. Fine hairs on the roots soak up water and minerals from the soil. These are **nutrients** that the plant needs.

The water and minerals mix in a sort of juice or sap. The juice travels up the plant's stem to the leaves. Leaves are use the energy in sunlight to turn water and other nutrients into food for the plant.

The roots of many plants have a third job. They store extra food that the plant does not need right away.

What's in Your Soil?

Soil is made up of many things. It may have chunky grains of sand. It may have dustlike bits of **silt.** It may have bits of rotted leaves and other decayed things. This is called **organic material.** Organic material is good for growing plants. It has lots of nutrients.

Soils from different places have different mixtures of these things. Here's how to find out what's in your soil.

What You Need:
- Clear jar or other container with a lid
- Soil
- Water

What to do:

- Put some soil in your jar.
- Fill the jar with water.
- Put on the lid. Shake well to mix the soil and water.
- Let the jar stand for a day. The different materials in the soil will settle in layers. Pebbles and sand will fall to the bottom. Silt will settle on top of the sand. Organic material will float at the top.
- Use a hand lens to study the layers. How much of each material does your soil have?

Do this activity again. Use a second jar, with soil from a different place. Compare the two samples. How are they different?

Seeds Grow in Soil

Most plants **reproduce** by making seeds. A seed is a little package. Inside its hard coat is a tiny plant, waiting to grow. The seed also has a store of food for the new plant.

The seeds scatter with the wind or in other ways. For growth to start, everything must be just right. The soil must be damp, but not too damp. It must be warm, but not too warm. Each kind of seed has different needs.

When a seed lands in the right spot, it will **sprout.** First it soaks up water from the soil. The water makes the seed swell. Its hard coat splits open. Then the little plant inside begins to grow. Tiny roots grow down into the soil from one end of the seed. From the other end, a little shoot grows up above the soil.

Dandelion seeds scatter in the wind.
Inset: When a seed lands in soil, it sprouts.

Grow Plants from Seeds

Many plants are easy to grow from seeds. You will have the best luck with seeds that you buy, rather than those you find outdoors. Many seeds grow best when started indoors in small pots.

What to do:

- Punch small holes in the bottoms of the containers. This will let extra water drain out.
- Fill the containers with potting soil.
- Place seeds in the soil. Different kinds of seeds must be planted at different depths. Follow the directions on the seed package.
- Sprinkle with water until the soil is evenly moist.
- Set the pots on a tray, to catch any water that leaks through. Keep them indoors in a warm, sunny place. Spray or sprinkle water on the soil whenever it begins to dry out.
- Seeds may take a week or more to sprout, depending on the kind of plant. When the new plants have several pairs of leaves, you can move them to the garden or to bigger pots.

7

Earthworms

Earthworms may seem icky and slimy. But they are good for soil. Like little magicians, they change dead plant material into rich new earth.
The worms eat bits of dead leaves and other rotting stuff. They break down this stuff into a sort of mush. Then they cast out their wastes. Earthworm castings are full of nutrients that plants need.

Below: An earthworm tunnels in the soil.
Inset: A worm pulls a dead leaf into its tunnel.

Earthworms help the soil in other ways. They wiggle through the earth to make tunnels. The worm's body has stiff bristles that it uses to pull itself along. Making tunnels helps turn and mix the soil. And the tunnels let air and water reach plant roots.

Earthworms dry out easily, so they hide in damp places. Their soft bodies are covered with slimy **mucus** that helps keep them from drying out. The mucus also helps the worm slide through the soil. The soil helps hide earthworms from birds and other animals that want to eat them. But sometimes birds find the worms anyway.

A young robin pulls a worm from the ground. Many birds eat worms.

World of Worms

You can watch earthworms make tunnels in this worm home.

To make a worm home:
- Put some gravel in the large container.
- Put cold water in the soda bottle. Place the bottle in the center of the container.
- Put a layer of damp soil around the bottle.
- Add a layer of damp sand. Keep adding layers of soil and sand up to a few inches from the top.
- Top with some damp leaves.
- Cover the outside with dark paper.

To find worms:
- Go on a worm hunt. Take a shovel and an empty coffee can or another container with high sides. Put wet paper towels in the bottom of the can.
- Use the shovel to turn over a leaf pile or some soil. If you see worms, scoop them up fast. They will wiggle away quickly! Carry them home in your can. Be sure to keep them moist.
- You can also buy worms. Check bait shops or sources such as those on page 24.

To watch the worms:

- Put the worms under the leaves in the worm home. Put the home in a cool place. Keep the paper cover on.
- The next day, take off the cover. What are the worms doing? Can you see their tunnels?
- Take a closer look. Put a worm on a damp paper towel. Mist it with water so it won't dry out. How does it move? What does it do when you touch it?

After a day or two, put the worms back where you found them. Cover them with soil or leaves.

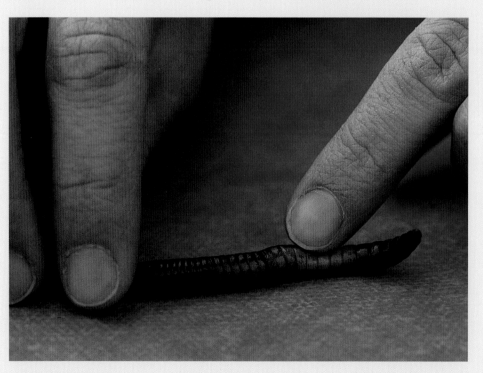

Insects in the Ground

Many kinds of insects live in the soil. Grubs burrow in the soil and eat plant roots. Grubs are the young, or **larvae,** of beetles. If grubs eat too many of a plant's roots, the plant will die.

Bumblebees nest in holes in the ground. During the day, bumblebees fly around looking for food. They visit flowers, gathering **pollen** and **nectar.** The bees turn nectar into honey and store it in the nest.

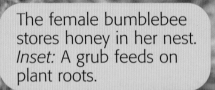

The female bumblebee stores honey in her nest. *Inset:* A grub feeds on plant roots.

12

A female called the queen bee starts the nest. She builds up a store of honey and pollen in a hole. Then she lays her eggs.

When the eggs hatch, larvae crawl out. They look like fat milky white worms. The larvae feed on honey and pollen. After a couple of weeks, they stop eating. They spin silky cocoons.

Inside their **cocoons,** the insects change. In about two weeks, they break out of the cocoons. Now they are adult bumblebees.

Bumblebee larvae change into adult bees inside cocoons. In the small picture, they look like fat worms. In the big picture, you can see the parts of an adult bee.

13

Ant Cities

An ant nest is like a city in the soil. The nest may be home to dozens or millions of ants.

The nest is made up of lots of rooms, linked by tunnels. The ants use some rooms for storing food that they bring back to the nest. Other rooms are for ant eggs or larvae. There are rooms where ants rest, too.

The entrance to the nest may be in the open or under a stone. Grains of soil may be piled around the entrance. The pile is called an anthill.

If an ant nest is disturbed, the ants will rush out. Some ants will try to defend their nests. And some will bite. Red fire ants give very painful bites! It's best to leave their nests alone.

Ants are always busy. *Top:* An ant takes an insect wing back to the nest. The wing will be food for the ants. *Center:* Ants gather around their queen in the nest. *Bottom:* An ant attacks a grasshopper that has landed on the nest.

Ant Alert

Ants are everywhere. In warm weather, you can see them in parks, backyards, fields, and woods. See if you can find an ant nest. Watch the ants come and go. When two ants meet, what do they do?

Use a hand lens to study an ant. How many sections does its body have? How many legs? Then find out what foods ants like.

What You Need:
- Heavy paper or cardboard
- Stones
- Bits of food—cookie, candy, fruit, vegetables, honey, or whatever else you have

What to do:
- Put the paper on the ground near an ant nest. Weight the corners with stones.
- Put bits of different foods on the paper.

Watch to see what the ants eat. Which foods do they like best?

15

Ant Lions

When you look for ants, you may find ant lions. These little insects dig pits in sandy soil. The pits are traps for ants and other **prey.**

The ant lion hides in the soil at the bottom of its pit. Only its big jaws stick out. An ant steps into the pit and tumbles to the bottom. The ant lion jumps out and grabs the ant in its jaws.

Ant lions eat other insects besides ants. They dig their pits in sand or dry, loose soil. An ant lion digs by pushing its tail end into the soil. It uses its head to flick soil out of the pit.

These digging insects are the larvae of a kind of fly. As adults, they look like small dragonflies. And they no longer trap ants.

An ant lion grabs an ant. *Inset:* An ant lion waits in its pit.

Keep an Ant Lion

What You Need:
- Shallow cup filled with sand
- Dark paper
- Ant lion

Ant lion larvae are easy to keep and fun to watch. Outside, look for pits in sandy soil. Scoop up the ant lion with a spoon. You can also buy ant lions by mail. See page 24 for a source.

Put the ant lion in an open container filled with clean sand. Watch it bury itself and dig its pit. Then do this to see how far it can toss sand.

What to do:
- Put dark paper on a table.
- Put the ant lion in the sand-filled cup. Then put the cup on the paper.
- Give the insect a day to make a pit. Then check to see how far it threw the sand.

If you put the ant lion back where you found it in a day or two, you will not need to feed it. If you keep it longer, feed it an ant or other small insect twice a week. Use tweezers to drop the ant in the pit.

Creepy Crawlers

Lots of other little animals live in and on the soil. A wolf spider may make its home under a rock or in a hole in the ground. The wolf spider does not spin a web. Instead, it hunts for the insects that it eats.

When a female wolf spider lays her eggs, she does not leave them, as most spiders do. She carries them with her, in a sac made of silk that she makes. When the eggs hatch, the little spiders climb on their mother's back. They ride around until they are old enough to be on their own.

Red velvet mites spend most of their time in the soil. You may see one on the surface after a rain. These mites are covered with fine red hair that looks like velvet.

This red velvet is about the size of this letter "o." The picture shows it larger than life.
Inset: A female wolf spider carries her eggs in a silk sac.

Red velvet mites are tiny. A big one might be the size of a pencil eraser. But these little mites bite and feed on insects that are much bigger than they are.

Centipedes also hunt for insect prey. They live under stones, in soil, and in rotting leaves. They can bite, so don't pick them up.

Spiders, mites, and centipedes may look like insects. But they are not insects. How can you tell? Count their legs! Insects always have six legs. Spiders and mites have eight legs. "Centipede" means "100 legs." But common centipedes have 30 legs, not 100.

Centipedes live under stones and logs. How many legs does this one have?

A star-nosed mole peeks out of its burrow in the soil.

At Home Underground

Larger animals live in the soil, too. Chipmunks, voles, and moles are **mammals.** They have fur. They give birth to live young. And the young feed on their mother's milk.

Chipmunks and voles dig burrows in the ground. They use the burrows to store food and to raise their young.

Moles are champion diggers. They tunnel just under the surface of the soil. That's where they find their favorite foods—grubs and earthworms.

Moles are small and sleek, with velvety fur. Their front feet are wide, with strong claws. The mole uses its claws to push soil out of the way as it digs. It seems to swim through the soil. Some moles can dig as fast as 1 foot (30 cm) a minute.

Moles have small eyes and ears. Eyes and ears are not very important in their dark world. A mole feels its way and finds its prey with its fleshy nose. The star-nosed mole has an amazing snout. Its nose has twenty-two wiggly pink arms.

Top: A chipmunk stores acorns and other nuts in its burrow. *Bottom:* A meadow vole digs under the roots of grass.

Words to Know

cocoon: a silk wrapping in which an insect changes into an adult

habitat: the place where a plant or animal naturally lives

larvae: the young forms of insects

mammals: animals that have fur, give birth to live young, and nurse their young with milk

mucus: a slimy substance made by glands in the body

nectar: a sweet liquid in flowers

nutrients: substances that a plant or animal needs to live

organic material: material that was once living

pollen: yellow powder made by flowers. It holds the plant's male sex cells.

prey: animals that are hunted by predators

reproduce: to make more of one's kind

silt: dustlike particles in soil

sprout: begin to grow

For More Information

Books

Eleanor Christian, et. al., *Looking at Ants.* Mankato, MN: Pebble Books, 2000.

John Farndon, *Life in the Soil.* San Diego: Blackbirch Press, 2004.

Allan Fowler, *Animals Under the Ground.* Danbury, CT: Childrens, 1998.

Carolyn B. Otto, *Spiders.* New York: Scholastic, 2002.

Wendy Pfeffer, *Wiggling Worms at Work.* New York: HarperCollins, 2003.

Patricia Whitehouse, *Moles.* Chicago, IL: Heinemann Library, 2004.

Websites

Ask the Answer Worm! (http://www.nrcs.usda.gov/feature/education/
squirm/skworm.html).
S. K. Worm, the official worm of the U.S. Department of Agriculture's
Natural Resources Conservation Service, answers students' questions about
soil.

Kidzone (www.nwf.org/kids).
This site from the National Wildlife Federation has information on wildlife
and habitats.

Sources

For earthworms:
Carolina Biological Supply Company
2700 York Road
Burlington, NC 27215
(800) 334-5551
www.carosci.com

Connecticut Valley Biological Supply
82 Valley Road, PO Box 326
Southampton, MA 01073
(800) 628-7748
www.ctvalleybio.com

For ant lions:
AntLionFarms.com
4509 Chantilly Way
Pensacola, FL 32505
(877) 332-8706
www.antlionfarms.com

Index